THE LITTLE BOOK OF BIG IDEAS

The Little Book of Big Ideas

First published in the UK by
New Internationalist Publications Ltd., Oxford, England.

Design by the New Internationalist.

Printed in China by C&C Offset Printing Co. Ltd.,

British Library Cataloguing-in-Publication Data.

A catalogue record for this book is available from the British Library.

ISBN 978-1-906523-21-3

New Internationalist Publications Ltd.
Registered Office: 55 Rectory Road, Oxford OX4 1BW

THE LITTLE BOOK OF

BIG IDEAS

Compiled by **Vanessa Baird**

New Internationalist

For my father

Foreword

Contrary to expectations a 'big idea' rarely if
ever springs pure and fully-formed from the
mind of one inspired genius. Even the
most original thinkers, to paraphrase Isaac
Newton, have 'seen further ahead by standing
on the shoulders' of their predecessors.

Ideas are such live, sparkling, dynamic
entities. Most are born not in solitude but as
a result of exchanges between people –
conversation, reading, experimentation, or
just swapping daydreams.

This is true in all fields, from astrophysics to
feminism. But there are certain individuals

who concentrate the ideas they assimilate and take them that bit further.

The result is theories, insights, and discoveries that may appear entirely new and full of energy.

These are the people whose names tend to appear at the bottom of the 'big ideas' featured in this book. Many are familiar household names – Gandhi, Einstein, Greer and Obama; others less so.

But all have something to say that is relevant to our times – which may perhaps spark off some 'big ideas' in readers too!

Vanessa Baird

Small is Beautiful

Small-scale operations, no matter how numerous, are always less likely to be harmful to the natural environment than large-scale ones, simply because their individual force is small in relation to the recuperative forces of nature. There is wisdom in smallness if only on account of the smallness and patchiness of human knowledge, which relies on experiment far more than on understanding. The greatest danger invariably arises from the ruthless application, on a vast scale, of practical knowledge such as we are currently witnessing in the application of nuclear energy, of the new chemistry in agriculture, of transportation technology, and countless other things.

EF Schumacher (1911-1977) German-born
radical economist and author of the
groundbreaking *Small is Beautiful*.

Women

One is not born, but rather becomes, a woman. No biological, psychological, or economic fate determines the figure that the human female presents in society; it is civilization as a whole that produces this creature... If, well before puberty and sometimes even from early infancy, she seems to us to be already sexually determined, this is not because mysterious instincts directly doom her to passivity, coquetry, maternity; it is because the influence of others upon the child is a factor almost from the start, and thus she is indoctrinated with her vocation from her earliest years.

Simone de Beauvoir (1908-1986),
French philosopher, feminist and author
of the groundbreaking *The Second Sex*.

Change

A new dawn of American leadership is at hand. To those who would tear this world down – we will defeat you. To those who seek peace and security – we support you. And to all those who have wondered if America's beacon still burns as bright – tonight we proved once more that the true strength of our nation comes not from the might of our arms or the scale of our wealth, but from the enduring power of our ideals: democracy, liberty, opportunity, and unyielding hope.

Barack Obama (b 1961),
first black US president.

Racial Equality

I have a dream that one day on the red hills of Georgia, the sons of former slaves and the sons of former slave-owners will be able to sit together at the table of brotherhood... that one day even the State of Mississippi, a state sweltering with the heat of injustice, sweltering with the heat of oppression, will be transformed into an oasis of freedom and justice... that my four little children will one day live in a nation where they will not be judged by the colour of their skin but by the content of their character.

Martin Luther King (1929-1968), US Civil Rights leader.

Land

None ought to be the lords or landlords over another, but the earth is free to every son and daughter of mankind to live free upon.

Gerard Winstanley, seventeenth century leader of the English revolutionary movement, the Diggers.

We Indian people are not supposed to say, this land is mine. We only use it. It is the white man who buys it and puts a fence around it. Indians are not supposed to do that, because the land belongs to all Indians, it belongs to God, as you call it. The land is a part of our body, and we are a part of the land.

Buffalo Tiger, contemporary, representative of the Miccosukee people of North America.

Class Struggle

The history of all hitherto existing society is the history of class struggles.

Freeman and slave, patrician and plebeian, lord and serf, guild-master and journeyman, in a word, oppressor and oppressed, stood in constant opposition to one another, carried on an uninterrupted, now hidden, now open fight, a fight that each time ended, either in a revolutionary reconstitution of society at large, or in the common ruin of the contending classes.

Karl Marx and Friedrich Engels (1818-1883 and 1820-1895), German political theorists, economists and authors of *The Communist Manifesto*.

Eco-feminism

The Age of Enlightenment, and the theory of progress to which it gave rise, was centred on the sacredness of two categories: modern scientific knowledge and economic development. Somewhere along the way, the unbridled pursuit of progress, guided by science and development, began to destroy life without any assessment of how fast or how much of the diversity of life on this planet is disappearing. Throughout the world... a new awareness is growing that is questioning the sanctity of science and development and revealing that these are not universal categories of progress, but the special projects of modern Western patriarchy... [In India] the everyday struggles of women for the protection of nature take place in the cognitive and ethical context... of an ancient Indian world-view in which nature is *Prakriti*, a living and creative process, the feminine principle from which all life arises.

Vandana Shiva, contemporary Indian physicist, philosopher, feminist and author of *Staying Alive*.

Action

Work for the elimination of concrete evils rather than for the realization of abstract goods. Do not aim at establishing happiness by political means. Rather aim at the elimination of poverty by direct means.

Karl Popper (1902-1994), Austrian-born philosopher and biochemist.

Globalization

The dream of the corporate empire builders is being realized. The global system is harmonizing standards across country after country – down toward the lowest common denominator. Although a few socially responsible businesses are standing against the tide with some limited success, theirs is not an easy struggle. We must not kid ourselves. Social responsibility is inefficient in the global free market, and the market will not long abuse those who do not avail of the opportunities to shed the inefficient. And we must be clear as to the meaning of efficiency. To the global economy, people are not only increasingly unnecessary, but they and their demands for a living wage are a major source of economic inefficiency. Global corporations are acting to purge themselves of this unwanted burden. We are creating a system that has fewer places for people.

David Korten, contemporary US economist and author of the influential *When Corporations Rule the World*.

Women's Emancipation

The right to vote will yet be swallowed up in the real question, viz: has a woman a right to herself? It is very little to me to have the right to vote, to own property etc. if I may not keep my body, and its uses, in my absolute right.

Lucy Stone, nineteenth century US
suffragette and editor.

Why is it that men's blood-shedding militancy is applauded and women's symbolic militancy punished with a prison-cell and the forcible feeding horror?

Emmeline Pankhurst (1858-1928), British suffragist.

Relativity

All motion is relative. We can never speak of absolute motion as such, but only motion relative to something else. In general, we cannot say that an object has a velocity of such-and-such, but must say it has a velocity of such-and-such relative to so-and-so. This is not done for objects on earth because it is understood that their velocities are relative to earth... But out away from the earth a velocity by itself has no meaning.

Albert Einstein (1879-1955), German-born physicist and originator of The Theory of Relativity, here paraphrased by James A Coleman.

Virtue

*T*o be able to practise five things everywhere under heaven constitutes perfect virtue... gravity, generosity of soul, sincerity, earnestness and kindness.

> **Confucius** (K'ung Fu Tzu, 551-479 BC), Chinese philosopher whose sayings are collected in the *Analects*.

*O*nly in our virtues are we original because virtue is difficult... Vices are general, virtues are particular.

> **Iris Murdoch** (1919-1999), Anglo-Irish moral philosopher and novelist.

Dreaming

Dreaming, in the sense of dreams, or the state between waking and deep sleep, is a state when revelations or instructions are received from the ancestors. Thus myths, songs and ceremonies are received in this state. This is the literal meaning, for the concept of Dreaming has been expanded into a deep spiritual and metaphysical concept, and in fact Dreaming and mythology may be seen as one and the same thing: the deep mental archetypes and wisdom images which we receive to guide us when the conscious mind is placed in a state of quiescence. Dreamings are those archetypes symbolized as ancestral beings, who came before and continue to live in the present generations. These eternal archetypes, sometimes equated with totems, are part of the spiritual identities of Aboriginal people.

Mudrooroo Nyoongah, contemporary Aboriginal novelist, poet, academic and author of *Aboriginal Mythology*.

Machines

Allow me the madness of inventing the future. The world which is upside down dreams that it lands on its feet.

In the streets, cars will be run over by dogs

The air will be free of all poisons of machines, and there will be

No other contamination than that which issues from human fear and passions

The television set will stop being the most important member of the family

And will be treated like the ironing board or the washing machine

Eduardo Galeano, contemporary Uruguayan writer, historian and author of *The Open Veins of Latin America.*

Machines are worshipped because they are beautiful and valued because they confer power; they are hated because they are hideous, and loathed because they impose slavery.

Bertrand Russell (1872-1970), British philosopher, mathematician and pacifist, author of *Sceptical Essays.*

Faith

I have found it necessary to deny knowledge in order to make room for faith.

Immanuel Kant (1724-1804),
German moral philosopher.

Violence

Some people draw a comforting distinction between 'force' and 'violence'... I refuse to cloud the issue by such word play... The power which establishes a state is violence; the power which maintains it is violence; the power which eventually overthrows it is violence... Call an elephant a rabbit only if it gives you comfort to feel that you are about to be trampled to death by a rabbit.

Kenneth Kaunda, contemporary, Zambian independence leader and former president.

World Citizenship

We are all citizens of the world, we are all of one blood. To hate a man because he was born in another country, because he speaks a different language, or because he takes a different view on this subject or that is a great folly. Desist, I implore you, for we are all equally human... Let us have but one end in view, the welfare of humanity.

John Comenius, seventeenth century writer and citizen of the world.

Food

I have come to see that food production and food distribution are in the midst of a revolution, a revolution that puts people's need for food last. And the revolution is led by the largest corporations on earth and élite-based governments. It is isn't fought in the name of liberty or equality or fraternity, but in the name of profit...

The outrage of hunger amidst plenty will never be solved by 'experts' somewhere. It will only be solved when people like you or me decide to act.

Frances Moore Lappé, contemporary, US co-founder of Food First and author of *World Hunger: Twelve Myths* and *Diet for a Small Planet*.

Enemies

Our most valuable teachers are our enemies. Not only is this a fundamental Buddhist teaching, it is a demonstrated fact of life. While our friends can help us in many ways, only our enemies can provide us with the challenge we need to develop tolerance, patience and compassion. These three virtues are essential for building character, developing peace of mind, and bringing us true happiness.

Tenzin Gyatso, contemporary Buddhist monk, the **Dalai Lama** and Tibetan leader in exile.

Natural Selection

Owing to this struggle for life any variation, however slight and from whatever cause proceding, if it be any degree profitable to an individual of any species, in its infinitely complex relations to other organic beings and to external nature, will tend to the preservation of that individual, and will generally be inherited by its offspring. The offspring also will thus have a better chance of surviving, for, of the many individuals of any species which are periodically born, but a small number can survive. I have called this principle, by which each slight variation, if useful, is preserved, by the term Natural Selection.

Charles Darwin (1809–1882), English natural historian, author of *Origin of Species* and *The Descent of Man*.

Passive Resistance

Passive resistance is an all-sided sword; it can be used anyhow; it blesses [one] who uses it and [one] against whom it is used without drawing a drop of blood; it produces far-reaching results. It never rusts and cannot be stolen. Competition between passive resisters does not exhaust them. The sword of passive resistance does not require a scabbard and one cannot be forcibly dispossessed of it.

Mohandas Karamchand (Mahatama) **Gandhi**
(1869-1948), Indian political leader and
social reformer.

Ease

Plan for the difficult while it is easy;
Act on the large while it's minute.

The most difficult things in the world
begin with things that are easy.

Laozi, a third century BC major text of Chinese
Taoism, whose precise authorship is unknown.

Nothing so saps the profound
resources of a life as finding life too
easy.

José Ortega Y Gasset (1883-1955),
Spanish philosopher and writer.

Communism

The theory of the Communists may be summed up in the single sentence: Abolition of private property.

Karl Marx and Friedrich Engels (1818-1883 and 1820-1895), German political theorists, economists and authors of *The Communist Manifesto*.

Life

Life can only be understood backwards but it must be lived forwards.

Søren Kierkegaard (1813-1855),
Danish philosopher, theologian
and founder of existentialism.

Oppression

In terms of historical function, there is a difference between revolutionary and reactionary violence, between violence practised by the oppressed and by the oppressors. In terms of ethics, both forms of violence are inhuman, and evil – but since when is history made in accordance with ethical standards? To start applying them at the point where the oppressed rebel against the oppressors, the have-nots against the haves, is serving the cause of actual violence by weakening the protests against it.

Herbert Marcuse (1898-1979), German-born American philosopher.

Ideals

On the day you kill me
You'll find in my pocket

Travel tickets

To peace,

To the fields and the rain,

To people's conscience.

Don't waste the tickets.

Samih al-Qasim, contemporary Palestinian poet.

Hope

I have cherished the ideal of a democratic and free society in which persons live together in harmony with equal opportunities. It is an ideal which I hope to live for, it is an ideal for which I am prepared to die.

Nelson Mandela, contemporary, South African Black liberation leader, who spent 30 years as a political prisoner and was President from 1994-1999.

Pessimism

Someone, who knows who, wrote in passing on a wall in the city of Bogotá: 'Let's leave pessimism for better times.'

Eduardo Galeano, contemporary Uruguayan writer, historian and author of *The Open Veins of Latin America*.

Responsibility

We see it like this: it is as if we are all in a canoe travelling through time. If someone begins to make a fire in their part of the canoe, and another begins to pour water inside the canoe, and another begins to piss in the canoe, it will affect us all. And it is the responsibility of each person in the canoe to ensure that it is not destroyed. Our planet is like one big canoe travelling through time.

Ailton Krenak, contemporary, activist with the Brazilian Union of Indian Nations (UNI).

The End of History

The soberest and most thoughtful minds of this century have seen no reason to think that the world is moving toward what we in the West consider decent and humane political institutions – that is liberal democracy. Our deepest thinkers have concluded that there is no such thing as History – that is, a meaningful order to the broad sweep of human events.... But if over time, more and more societies with diverse cultures and histories exhibit similar long terms patterns of development; if there is a continuing convergence in the types of institutions governing most advanced societies; and if the homogenization of mankind continues as a result of economic development, then the idea of relativism may seem much stranger than it does now. For the apparent differences between peoples... will be an artefact of their particular stage of human development.

Francis Fukuyama, contemporary, US conservative, libertarian political theorist and author of *The End of History* and the Last Man.

Poverty

There were two 'Reigns of Terror' [in revolutionary France], if we could but remember and consider it; the one wrought murder in hot passions, the other in heartless cold blood; the one lasted mere months, the other had lasted a thousand years; the one inflicted death upon a thousand persons, the other upon a hundred million; but our shudders are for the horrors of the minor terror, the momentary Terror, so to speak; whereas, what is the horror of swift death by axe compared with lifelong death from hunger, cold, insult, cruelty and heartbreak.

Mark Twain (1835-1910), US writer, wit and author.

Poetry and Freedom

The white fathers told us: 'I think, therefore I am' and the black woman within each of us – the poet – whispers in our dreams, I feel, therefore I can be free. Poetry coins the language to express and charter this revolutionary demand.

Audre Lorde (1934-1992), US writer, feminist and author of *Zami: a new spelling of my name.*

Community

They were nothing more than people, by themselves. Even paired, any pairing, they would have been nothing more than people by themselves. But all together, they had become the heart and muscles and mind of something perilous and new, something strange and growing and great. Together, all together, they were instruments of change.

Keri Hulme, contemporary Maori author and painter, writing in *The Bone People.*

Gaia Theory

Gaia is the earth seen as a single physiological system, an entity that is alive at least to the extent that, like other living organisms, its chemistry and temperature are self-regulated at a state favourable for life... I describe Gaia as a control system for the Earth – a self-regulating system something like the familiar thermostat of a domestic iron or oven... [It is] an evolving system, a system made up of all living things and their surface environment, the oceans, atmosphere, and crystal rocks, the two parts tightly coupled and indivisible. It is an 'emergent domain' – a system that has emerged from the reciprocal evolution of organisms and their environment over the aeons of life on Earth. No foresight, planning, or teleology (suggestion of design or purpose in nature) are involved.

James Lovelock, contemporary British scientist-philosopher, originator of the Gaia hypothesis, author of *Gaia: the practical science of planetary medicine*.

Death

Death is an evil; the gods have so judged it; had it been good, they would die.

Sappho (c 610-635 BC) lyric poet from the Greek island of Lesbos.

Racism

I am over-determined from without, I am the slave not of the 'idea' that others have of me but of my own appearance...

Shame. Shame and self-contempt. Nausea. When people like me, they tell me it is in spite of my colour. When they dislike me, they point out that it is not because of my colour. Either way I am locked into the infernal circle.

Frantz Fanon (1915-1961), Martinique-born critic of colonialism, key figure in Algeria's struggle for independence and author of *Black Skin, White Masks*.

Memory

A bad memory is an advantage to its owner but injurious to... descendants. The ability to forget the past enables people to free themselves gradually from the pain they once suffered; but it also often makes them repeat the mistakes of their predecessors.

Lu Xun (1881-1936), outspoken Chinese essayist.

Consent

The process of creating and entrenching highly selective, reshaped or completely fabricated memories of the past is what we call 'indoctrination' or 'propaganda' when it is conducted by official enemies, and 'education', 'moral instruction' or 'character building' when we do it ourselves. It is a valuable mechanism of control, since it effectively blocks any understanding of what is happening in the world. One crucial goal of successful education is to deflect attention elsewhere... and away from our own institutions and their systematic functioning and behaviour, the real source of a great deal of the violence and suffering in the world. It is crucially important to prevent understanding and to divert attention from the sources of our own conduct, so that élite groups can act without popular constraints to achieve their goals – which are called 'the national interest'.

Noam Chomsky, contemporary, US linguistics and political theorist, essayist and author of *Manufacturing Consent*.

Ideas

To die for an idea is to place a pretty high price upon conjectures.

Anatole France (1844-1924), French novelist and critic.

Ideas have unhinged the gates of empires.

Paul L Harris, contemporary, US academic.

Don't worry about people stealing your ideas. If your ideas are any good, you'll have to ram them down people's throats.

Howard Aiken (1900-1973), a pioneer in computing.

Ideas

Great ideas come into the world as quietly as doves. Perhaps then, if we listen attentively we shall hear, among the uproar of empires and nations, the faint fluttering of wings, the gentle stirrings of life and hope. Some will say this hope lies in a nation; others in a man. I believe rather that it is awakened, revived, nourished by millions of solitary individuals whose deeds and works every day negate frontiers and the crudest implications of history. Each and every one, on the foundations of their own suffering and joy builds for all.

Albert Camus (1913-1960), Algerian-born French author.

Freedom

Freedom is not choosing: that is merely the move that we all make when all is already lost. Freedom is knowing and understanding and respecting things quite other than ourselves.

Iris Murdoch (1919-1999), Anglo-Irish moral philosopher, novelist and author of *The Sublime and the Beautiful Revisited*.

Those who deny freedom to others deserve it not for themselves.

Abraham Lincoln (1809-1865), US President, lawyer and abolitionist.

Personal Politics

One of the simplest and most disturbing feminist insights is that 'the personal is political'. Disturbing because it means that relationships we once imagined were private or merely social are in fact infused with power, usually unequal power backed up by public authority. Rape, therefore, is about power more than it is about sex, and not only the rapist but the state is culpable... But the assertion that the 'personal is political' is one of those phrases that can be read backwards as well as forwards. Read 'the political is personal', it suggests that politics is not shaped merely by what happens in legislative debates, voting booths and war rooms. While men, who dominate public life, have told women to stay in the kitchen, they have used their public power to construct private relationships in ways that bolstered their masculinized political control.

Cynthia Enloe, contemporary US feminist academic, writer and critic of militarism.

Education

Democracy and democratic education are founded on faith in people, on the belief that they not only can but should discuss the problems of their country, of their continent, their world, their work, the problems of democracy itself. Education is an act of love, and thus an act of courage. It cannot fear the analysis of reality or, under pain of revealing itself as a farce, avoid creative discussion.

Paulo Freire (1921-1997), radical Brazilian educator and author of *Pedagogy of the Oppressed*.

Economics

What a country calls its vital economic interests are not the things which enable its citizens to live, but the things which enable it to make war; petrol is much more likely than wheat to be a cause of international conflict.

Simone Weil (1909-1943), French philosopher, mystic, humanitarian and revolutionary.

Language

It may not be easy to break out of the patterns of thinking and believing into which our society and language have led us, but it is possible. Language is a human product, it is something which human beings have made, and which can be modified. We can – with perseverance – posit alternatives to those which are readily available within our society. We can make the efforts to formulate possibilities at the periphery of our cultural conditioning – and we can validate them... If and when sufficient women agree that they no longer subscribe to the rules and patterns of patriarchy, then the rules and patterns are likely to be transformed...

Dale Spender, contemporary Australian feminist, academic and author of *Man Made Language.*

Self-confidence

And he said: you pretty full of yourself ain't chu

So she replied: show me someone not full of herself and i'll show you a hungry person.

Nikki Giovanni, contemporary US poet and writer.

Aspiration

Earth, old man of the planets, you suck at my foot which wants to fly.

Nelly Sachs (1891-1969), German-born Swedish poet and playwright.

Atomic energy

It is customary to express the equivalence of mass and energy... by the formula $E = mc^2$, in which c represents the velocity of light, about 186,000 miles per second. E is the energy that is contained in a stationary body; m is its mass. The energy that belongs to the mass m is equal to this mass, multiplied by the square of the enormous speed of light – which is to say, a vast amount of energy for every unit of mass.

But if every gram of material contains this tremendous energy, why did it go so long unnoticed? The answer is simple enough: so long as none of the energy is given off externally, it cannot be observed... We know only one sphere in which such amounts of energy per mass are released: namely radioactive disintegration...

Albert Einstein (1879-1955), German-born physicist whose famous formula $E = mc^2$ ultimately led to nuclear power and weapons.

Superstition and Truth

[Humans] will fight for a superstition quite as quickly as for a living thing, truth – often more so, since a superstition is so intangible you cannot get at it to refute it, but truth is a point of view, and so is changeable.

Hypatia (c 370-415 BC),
Greek philosopher and scientist.

Radiation

I came to treat as many as twenty kilograms of [the new radioactive substance] at the time which had the effect of filling the shed with great jars of precipitates and liquids. It was killing work to carry such receivers, to pour off the liquids and to stir for hours at a stretch the boiling matter in a smelting basin...

It contains a new element to which we propose to give the name RADIUM.

Marie Curie (1867-1934), Polish-born French physicist who in 1898, with her husband Pierre, discovered radium, making possible the medical use of radiation.

Inferiority

No one can make you feel inferior without your consent.

Eleanor Roosevelt (1884-1962), social reformer and US 'First Lady'.

Medicine

Sometimes give your services for nothing... And if there be an opportunity of serving one who is a stranger in financial straits, give full assistance to all such. For where there is love of human beings there is also love of the art.

Hippocrates (460-377 BC) Greek physician who founded a school of medicine where all students were required to take an oath and observe a code of practice putting patients' interests above all others.

Capitalism

*C*apitalist production develops technology solely by sapping the original sources of all wealth – the soil and the labourer.

...and its end...

The centralization of the means of production and socialization of labour reach a point where they prove incompatible with the capitalist husk. This bursts asunder. The expropriators are expropriated.

Karl Marx (1818-1883), German political theorist writing in *Das Kapital*.

Chaos

The vision given to us by Newton and... the Age of Enlightenment is of an orderly and predictable world, governed by laws and rules which can best be expressed in mathematical form... Effectively unpredictable situations were thought to arise only because the rules were many and complicated... This vision has splintered... It is now widely understood that the simplest rules or algorithms or mathematical equations, containing no random elements whatsoever, can generate behaviour which is as complicated as anything we can imagine. This is the mathematics of 'deterministic chaos'... one of the real revolutions in the way we think about the world. Knowing the simple rule or equation that governs a system is not always sufficient to predict its behaviour. And conversely, exceedingly complicated patterns of behaviour may derive... from the chaotic workings of some very simple algorithm.

Robert May, a pioneer of chaos theory, which has been traced back to a 1963 paper by US meteorologist Edward Lorenz.

Youth

Gentle ladies, you will remember till old age what we did together in our brilliant youth!

Sappho (c 610-635 BC) lyric poet from the Greek island of Lesbos.

No wise man ever wished to be younger.

Jonathan Swift (1667-1745), Irish satirist, essayist, poet, pamphleteer and Anglican cleric.

Security

*W*e need a wider definition of national security... The destruction of the planet's environment is making the world a less stable place, politically, economically and militarily... Our environmental management practices have focused largely upon after-the-fact repair of damage... The ability to anticipate and prevent environmental damage will require that the ecological dimensions of policy be considered at the same time as the economic, trade, energy, agricultural and other dimensions.

Gro Brundtland, contemporary Norwegian politician and former leader, renowned for her international commitment to environmentalism.

Revolutionaries

The duty of every revolutionary is to make a revolution.

Fidel Castro, revolutionary hero and Cuban leader from 1959 to 2008.

Every revolutionary ends by becoming either an oppressor or a heretic.

Albert Camus (1913-1960), French novelist, essayist and playwright.

Violence

It's politely assumed that democracy is a means of containing and restraining violence. But violence comes not from genes but from ideas.

Edward Bond (b 1934), UK playwright.

Cyberspace

A consensual hallucination experienced daily by millions of legitimate operators, in every nation... A graphic representation of data abstracted from the bank of every computer in the human system. Unthinkable complexity. Lines of light ranged in the nonspace of the mind, clusters and constellations of data. Like city lights receding.

William Gibson, US science fiction writer and originator of the term 'Cyberspace' in his 1984 classic *Neuromancer*.

Honesty

Better to live as a rogue and a bum

a lover all treat as a joke

to hang out with a crowd of

comfortable drunks

than to crouch in a hypocrite's cloak.

Mahsati, twelfth century Iranian woman poet.

The Collective Unconscious

In addition to our immediate consciousness, which is of a thoroughly personal nature and which we believe to be the only empirical psyche, there exists a second psychic system of a collective, universal, and impersonal nature which is identical in all individuals. This collective unconscious does not develop individually but is inherited. It consists of pre-existent forms, the archetypes, which can only become conscious secondarily and which give definite form to certain psychic contents.

Carl G Jung (1875-1961), Swiss psychologist, prolific author and originator of *The Concept of the Collective Unconscious.*

Action and Reaction

To every action there is always an equal reaction: or, the mutual actions of two bodies upon each other are always equal, and directed to contrary parts.

Isaac Newton (1642-1727), British physicist and mathematician, who laid the foundation for modern physics.

Love

To fear love is to fear life; and those that fear life are already three parts dead.

Bernard Russell (1872-1970), British philosopher and mathematician, writing in *Marriage and Morals*.

Love, love love – all the wretched cant of it, masking egotism, lust, masochism, fantasy under a mythology of sentimental postures.

Germaine Greer, contemporary Australian-born feminist, author of *The Female Eunuch*.

Love one another, but make not a bond of love: Let it rather be a moving sea between the shores of your souls.

Kahlil Gibran (1883-1931), Lebanese poet, mystic, painter and author of *The Prophet*.

Race

My issue is race. I feel black people nowadays have to conform to this one ideal. We all have to be the same. We all have to be hard and ghetto and listen to only one genre of music which would be Rap and R&B. And if one of us steps out of the mould we're not black anymore. Well, that's dumb. When did music determine your racial background?

Kamanda Ndama (b 1989), African musician and poet.

Hell

*T*he infliction of cruelty with a good conscience is a delight to moralists. That is why they invented Hell.

Bertrand Russell (1872-1970), British philosopher, mathematician and pacifist, writing in *Sceptical Essays*.

*S*o that's what hell is. I'd never have believed it... Do you remember, brimstone, the stake, the gridiron.... What a joke! No need of a gridiron, Hell is other people.

Jean-Paul Sartre (1905-1980), French philosopher, novelist, playwright and essayist, writing in *In Camera*.

Limitations

If we forgive God for his crime against us, which is to have made us finite creatures, he will forgive our crime against him, which is that we are finite creatures.

Simone Weil (1909-1943), French philosopher, mystic, humanitarian, revolutionary.

Sexual Orientation

Those of us who are forged in the crucibles of difference know that survival is not an academic skill.

Audre Lorde, (1934-1992), US poet, novelist, essayist and author of *Sister Outsider*.

No government has the right to tell its citizens when or whom to love. The only queer people are those who don't love anybody.

Rita Mae Brown, contemporary US writer and author of *Ruby Fruit Jungle*.

For me it's a matter of human rights and a deeply theological issue.

Archbishop Desmond Tutu, contemporary, South African church leader who has described discrimination against homosexuals as 'unjust as apartheid'.

Economic Centralism

We the workers, shall organize large scale production on the basis of what capitalism has already created, relying on our own experience as workers, establishing strict, iron discipline backed by state power of the armed workers. We shall reduce the role of state officials to that of simply carrying out our instructions as responsible, revocable, modestly paid 'foremen and accountants...'

Vladimir Ilyich Lenin (1870-1924),
Russian Communist leader and theorist.

Reality

I do not know whether I was a man dreaming I was a butterfly, or whether I am now a butterfly dreaming I am a man.

Chuang Tse (c 369-286 BC),
Chinese Taoist philosopher.

Universal Rights

Where, after all, do universal human rights begin? In small places, close to home – so close and so small that they cannot be seen on any maps of the world. Yet they are the world of the individual persons; the neighbourhood [one] lives in; the school or college [one] attends; the factory, farm or office where [one] works. Such are the places where every man, woman and child seeks equal justice, equal opportunity, equal dignity without discrimination. Unless these rights have meaning there, they have little meaning anywhere. Without concerned citizen action to uphold them close to home, we shall look in vain for progress in the larger world.

Eleanor Roosevelt (1884-1962),
social reformer and US 'First Lady'.

Gentleness

If you catch hold of a cat by its tail, it will bite you. The world will do the same. Live in the world like water on a lotus leaf.

Yogaswami (1872 -1964), Sri Lankan spiritual leader, influenced by Hinduism.

Labels

All reduction of people to objects, all imposition of labels and patterns to which they must conform, all segregation can lead only to destruction.

> **Maureen Duffy,** contemporary British writer, playwright and author of *As it was*

Bringing down Civilization

People say 'what do you mean when you talk about "bringing down civilization"?'. What I really mean is depriving the rich of the ability to steal from the poor and depriving the powerful of the ability to destroy the planet. That's what I really mean.

> **Derrick Jensen** (b 1960), US environmental activist and writer.

Creation

In the beginning God created the heaven and the earth. And the earth was without form, and void; and darkness was upon the face of the deep. And the Spirit of God moved upon the face of the waters. And God said, Let there be light: and there was light. And God saw the light, and it was good; and God divided the light from the darkness. And God called the light Day, and the darkness he called Night. And the evening and the morning were the first day.

The First Book of Moses, called Genesis.

There has been no creation. How can there be 'the beginning'? The creation is continuous: it is creativity. Back you move, you will not find the beginning, ahead you go, you will not find the end. It is beginningless, endless creative energy. So in the first place there was no beginning. God never created the world – there is no God.

Osho aka Bhagwan Shree Rajneesh (1931-1990),
Indian mystic.

Animals

There is no ethical basis for elevating membership of one particular species into a morally crucial characteristic. From an ethical point of view, we all stand on an equal footing – whether we stand on two feet, one foot, or none at all...

Peter Singer, contemporary Australian moral philosopher, writing in *Animal Liberation*.

The question is not, can they reason? Nor, can they talk? But can they suffer? Why should the law refuse protection to any sensitive being?

Jeremy Bentham (1748-1832), British Utilitarian philosopher writing in *Principles of Morals and Legislation*.

Laughter

Life does not cease to be funny when people die, any more than it ceases to be serious when people laugh.

George Bernard Shaw (1856-1950), Irish dramatist, essayist and Fabian Socialist.

Socialism

Socialism can only arrive by bicycle.

José Antonio Viera Gallo, contemporary, Chilean assistant Secretary of Justice in Allende's government.

The truth is that a conception of Socialism which views it as involving the nationalization of everything except political power, on which all else depends, is not, to speak with moderation, according to light. The question is not merely whether the State owns and controls the means of production. It is also, who owns and controls the State?

Richard Tawney (1880-1962), British economic historian and political theorist

Liberation

It's as if we think liberation is a fixed quantity, that there is only so much to go around. That an individual or community is liberated at the expense of another. When we view liberation as a scarce resource, something only a precious few of us can have, we stifle our potential, our creativity, our genius for living, learning and growing.

Andrea Canaan, contemporary, US poet and writer.

Political Rhetoric

Political language – and with variations this is true of all political parties – is designed to make lies sound truthful and murder respectable.

> **George Orwell** (1903-1950), English novelist and essayist, in the *Politics of the English Language*.

Politicians are the same everywhere. They promise to build a bridge even when there's no river.

> **Nikita Khrushchev** (1894-1977), Soviet president, and denouncer of Stalin.

War and Peace

There never was a good war, or a bad peace.

Benjamin Franklin (1706-1790),
American independence leader.

Awareness

Our attention is to affirm this life, not to bring order out of a chaos nor to suggest improvements in creation, but simply to wake up to the very life we're living, which is so excellent once one gets one's mind and one's desires out of its way and lets it act of its own accord.

John Cage (1912 -1992), US radical composer and musical theorist.

Repression

There are characteristic features attributed to repression, which serve to distinguish it from prohibitions maintained by penal law: repression operated as a sentence to disappear, but also as an injunction to silence, an affirmation of non-existence, and, by implication, an admission that there was nothing to say about such things, nothing to see, nothing to know.

Michel Foucault (1926-1984), French social scientist and historian of ideas.

Heaven

Heaven is where all the interesting people are missing.

Freidrich Nietzsche (1844-1900),
German philosopher and author
of *Thus Spake Zarathustra*.

Culture

Letting a thousand flowers blossom and a hundred schools of thought contend is the policy for promoting the progress of the arts and sciences.

Mao Zedong (1893-1976), Chinese revolutionary leader, whose words and actions rarely coincided, in *The Quotations of Chairman Mao Tse Tung*.

Nature

The 'control of nature' is a phrase conceived in arrogance, born of a Neanderthal age of biology and philosophy, when it was supposed that nature exists for the convenience of humans. The concepts and practices of applied entomology for the most part date from that Stone Age science. It is our alarming misfortune that so primitive a science has armed itself with the most modern and terrible weapons, and that in turning them against the insects it has also turned them against the earth.

Rachel Carson (1907-1964), US genetic biologist and author of the classic text of the ecology movement, *Silent Spring*.

Devotion

I have felt the swaying of the elephant's shoulders ....

and now you want me to climb on a jackass? Try to be serious!

Mira Bai (1498-1547), Indian Hindu mystic, poet and princess, who renounced all worldly goods.

Computers

It is desirable to guard against the possibility of exaggerated ideas that might arise as to the powers of the Analytical Engine. The Analytical Engine has no pretensions whatsoever to originate anything. It can do whatever we know to order it to perform. It can follow analysis; but it has no power of anticipating any analytical relations or truths. Its province is to assist us in making available what we are already acquainted with. That it is calculated to effect primarily and chiefly of course, through its executive faculties; but is likely to exert an indirect and reciprocal influence on science itself in another manner. For, in so distributing and combining the truths and the formulae of analysis, that they may come more easily and rapidly amenable to the mechanical combinations of the engine, the relations and the nature of many subjects in that science are necessarily thrown into new lights, and more profoundly investigated...

Ada Lovelace (1815-1852), British mathematician who predicted the computer or 'analytical engine' and devised mathematical programs for it.

Progress

We have for over a century been dragged behind the chariot of the prosperous West, choked by the dust, deafened by the noise, humbled by our own helplessness and overwhelmed by the speed. We agreed to acknowledge that this chariot drive was progress, and progress was civilization. If we ever ventured to ask, 'progress towards what, or progress for whom?' it was considered ridiculously oriental to entertain such ideas about the absoluteness of progress. Of late, a voice has come to us to take count not only of the scientific perfection of the chariot but of the depth of the ditches lying in its path.

Rabindranath Tagore (1861-1941), Indian poet.

The unexamined life is not a life worth living for a human being.

Socrates (469-399 BC), Greek philosopher,
quoted in *Plato's Apology*.

Struggle

The battles that count aren't the ones for gold medals. The struggles within yourself – the invisible, inevitable battles inside all of us – that's where it's at.

Jesse Owens (1913-1980), US Olympian gold medalist.

Class

The central socialist ideal is equality. By this I do not mean identical incomes or uniform habits and tastes. But I do mean a classless society – one in which relations between all people are similar to those hitherto existing within one social class; one in which though there are differences between individuals there are no feelings or attitudes of superiority and inferiority between groups; one in which although some jobs are paid more than others, the differentials are based on generally acceptable criteria – skill, responsibility, effort, danger, dirt; one in which though people develop differently, there is equal opportunity for all to develop.

Hugh Gaitskell (1906-1963),
British Labour Party leader.

Genetic Determinism

They are in you and in me; they created us, body and mind; and their preservation is the ultimate rationale for our existence... they go by the name of genes and we are their survival machines.

Richard Dawkins (b 1941), British biologist and author of *The Selfish Gene* and *The God Delusion*.

Religion

We have just enough religion to make us hate, but not enough to make us love each other.

Jonathan Swift (1667-1745), Irish satirist, essayist, poet, pamphleteer and Anglican cleric.

Let there be no violence in religion.

The Koran, seventh century.

Religion is the sigh of the oppressed creating the feelings of a heartless world and the spirit of conditions that are unspiritual. It is the opium of the people.

Karl Marx (1818-1883), German political theorist, writing in the *Preface to a Critique of Hegel's Philosophy of Right*.

Beauty and Utility

If you want one golden rule that will fit everybody, this is it: have nothing in your houses that you do not know to be useful, or believe to be beautiful.

William Morris (1834-1896), English writer, designer and socialist.

Property

If I were asked the following question: 'What is slavery?' and I replied in one word 'Murder!' my meaning would be understood at once... Why then, to this other question: 'What is property?' may I not likewise answer, 'Theft'?

Pierre-Joseph Proudhon (1809-1865), French social reformer and anarchist, politician and writer imprisoned for his beliefs, writing in *Qu'est-ce que la propriété?*

Simplicity

How many things I have no need of!

Socrates (469-399 BC), Greek philosopher.

Political struggle

Each new rising and new victory of the political struggle simultaneously changes itself into a powerful impetus for the economic struggle by expanding the external possibilities of the latter, increasing the inner drive of the workers to better their situation and increasing their desire to struggle. After each new foaming wave of political action a fructifying deposit remains behind from which a thousand stalks of economic struggle shoot forth. And vice versa. The ceaseless state of economic war of the workers with capital keeps alive the fighting energy of every political cause. It forms, so to speak, the ever-fresh reservoir of strength of the proletarian class, out of which the political struggle continually renews its strength.

Rosa Luxemberg (1870-1919), Polish-born German revolutionary and socialist.

Pleasure

I shouldn't be surprised if the greatest rule of all weren't to give pleasure.

Molière (1622-1673), French comic playwright.

Sickness and Health

Illness is the night-side of life, a more onerous citizenship. Everyone who is born holds dual citizenship, in the kingdom of the well and in the kingdom of the sick. Although we all prefer to use only the good passport, sooner or later each of us is obliged, at least for a spell, to identify ourselves as citizens of that other place.

Susan Sontag (1933-2004), US Critic essayist, novelist and short story writer, writing in *Illness as Metaphor*.

Sustainable Growth

It is impossible for the world economy to grow its way out of poverty and environmental degradation... In its physical dimensions, the economy is an open subsystem of the earth's ecosystem, which is finite, non growing and materially closed. Therefore its growth is not sustainable. The term sustainable growth when applied to the economy is a bad oxymoron – self-contradiction as prose and unevocative as poetry.

Herman E Daly, contemporary, US economics professor and pioneer critic of the validity of conventional economics.

Prison

Jails and prisons are designed to break human beings, to convert the population into specimens in a zoo – obedient to our keepers, but dangerous to each other.

Angela Davis, contemporary, US activist and writer.

Indigenous Knowledge

In searching for the new environmental and social order we should realize that it is in the Third World that the new ecologically sound societies will be born. Within each Third World nation there are still large areas where communities earn their livelihoods in ways that are consistent with the preservation of their culture and their natural environment. Such communities have nearly disappeared in the developed world. We need to recognize and rediscover the technological and cultural wisdom of our indigenous systems of agriculture, industry, shelter, water and sanitation, and medicine.

Martin Khor, contemporary, Malaysian president of the Third World Network in Penang.

Money

Above all things good policy is to be used, that the treasure and money in a state be not gathered into few hands. For otherwise a state may have a great stock, and yet starve. And money is like muck, not good except it be spread. This is done chiefly by suppressing, or at least keeping a strait hand upon, the devouring trades of usury, ingrossing, great pasturages, and the like.

Francis Bacon (1561-1626), English philosopher and essayist in *Essays Moral and Civil*.

Money can't buy friends, but you can get a better class of enemy

Spike Milligan (1918-2002), British comic, writing in *Puckoon*.

Psychoanalysis

In psychoanalysis... everything is different. Nothing takes place in psychoanalytic treatment but an exchange of words between the patient and the analyst. The patient talks, tells of... past experiences and present impressions, complains, confesses wishes and... emotional responses. The doctor listens, tries to direct the patient's processes of thought, exhorts, gives... explanations and observes the reaction of understanding or rejection... The uninstructed relatives of our patients, who are impressed only by visible and tangible things... never fail to express their doubts whether 'anything can be done about an illness by mere talking'. That, of course, is both short-sighted and an inconsistent line of thought. These are the same people who are so certain that patients are 'simply imagining' their symptoms. Words were originally magic and to this day words have retained much of their ancient magical power.

Sigmund Freud (1856-1939), Austrian
founder of psychoanalysis, in
Introductory Lectures on Psychoanalysis.

Anarchy

Where the State begins individual freedom ends...

Michael Bakunin (1814-1876), Russian anarchist.

There's no reason why a society consisting of rational beings capable of empathizing with each other, complete and having no natural reason to compete, should have a government, laws, or leaders.

Valerie Solanas (1936-1988), US separatist feminist.

Reconciliation

We blacks for our part are ready to forgive, but the other party must be contrite and ready to make reparation to demonstrate the seriousness of their contrition, and then reconciliation can happen. You cannot say you are sorry you stole my pen if you continue to retain possession of it.

Archbishop Desmond Tutu, contemporary, South African Anglican church leader and chair of South Africa's Truth and Reconciliation commission.

Exchange

Money is really just an immaterial measure, like an inch, or a gallon, a pound or degree. While there is certainly a limit on real resources – only so many hours in a day – there need never be a shortage of measure... yet this is precisely the situation in which we persist in regarding money. Money is, for the most part, merely a symbol, accepted to be valuable generally throughout the society that uses it. Why should we ever be short of symbols to keep account of how we serve one another?

Michael Linton, contemporary, Canadian creator of the Local Exchange Trading Scheme (LETS) in British Columbia in 1983.

Sense of Place

One has to develop a relationship with a certain place, where the land knows you, and experience that the trees, the Earth and nature are extending their love and light to you, to know there is so much we can receive from the Earth, to fill our hearts and souls...

Inti Velasquez, contemporary, Inca Shaman in Peru.

Big Bang

These days most cosmologists and astronomers back the theory that there was indeed a creation, about eighteen billion years ago, when the physical universe burst into existence in an awesome explosion popularly known as the 'big bang'.

Paul Davies, contemporary, scientist and author of *God and the New Physics*.

Strength

We are only small – very few thousand people out there on tiny islands, but we are doing our part to stop this nuclear madness. And although we are few we have done it. Which means you can do it too.

Darlene Leju-Johnson, contemporary, Marshall Islander and campaigner for a nuclear-free and independent Pacific.

Natural Rights

We must go beyond the arrogance of human rights. We must go beyond the ignorance of civil rights. We must step into the reality of natural rights because all the natural world has a right to existence. We are only a small part of it. There can be no trade off.

John Trudell, contemporary, Native American singer, songwriter and activist.

Energy

A peace treaty between humankind and nature is not possible without a global solar energy economy. We are very pressed for time but, on the other hand, we have the opportunities for a solar strategy within our grasp and have reached the point where we should no longer bear with the inhuman delaying tactics of those who 'don't do what they know must be done'. To use the 'energy of the people' we need to mobilize people's energies – to stir up a solar energy revolution.

> **Hermann Scheer**, contemporary,
> German founder of Eurosolar,
> and author of *A Solar Manifesto*.

It is not clear, apart from inertia, ignorance and institutional complacency, what the obstacles are to energy efficiency.

> **Michael Jefferson,** contemporary,
> World Energy Council.

Oneness

I believe the world has moved closer to oneness and more people see each other as one with the other... It is possible to have new thoughts and new common values for humans and all other forms of life...

Wangari Maathai, contemporary, co-ordinator of the Kenya Green Belt movement.

Rebelliousness

People ask me why I'm so rebellious. Well, I don't think I'm being a rebel. People perceive that being rebellious is a bad thing, but if fighting for what I believe in is being rebellious, I am a rebel. But I think you are the rebels; you're the ones rebelling against the peace, love, and unity I am trying to promote. I think you are rebelling against mankind. You racist, You anti-life war-makers. I believe you are rebelling against the human race.

Kamanda Ndama (b 1989), African musician and poet.

Background

Contempt for background impresses me as little as pride in background. Both are distorting. Tormented, self-regarding resolutions·of cultural conflict create new, tormenting problems.

Nissim Ezekiel (1924-2004), Jewish Indian poet.

People

Yes, because as long as you go on defending the country, you go on killing – others, and yourself. You see, the defence of country has absolutely nothing to do with the defence of people. Once we get rid of the obsession with defending one's country we will begin defending life. We will begin to have a real sense of what it's like to take care of people instead of trying to watch over a piece of land.

Joan Baez, contemporary, US singer and human-rights activist.

Domination

So kings find it odd they should have a million subjects

Yet share in the thoughts of none, and seducers

Are sincerely puzzled at being unable to love

What they are able to possess.

WH Auden (1907-1973), British poet.

Delight

X once told me that love had protected him against worldliness: coteries, ambitions, advancements, interferences, alliances, secessions, roles, powers: love had made him into a social catastrophe, to his delight.

Roland Barthes (1915-1980), French cultural critic.

Resistance

It's happening in many places on the Latin American map: people are uniting against the paralyzing gases of fear and, united, they are learning not to bow their heads. As Old Antonio says: 'Everyone is as small as the fear they feel, and as big as the enemy they choose.'

Eduardo Galeano, contemporary, Uruguayan historian and author of *Memory of Fire.*

Sex

Love-making is never simply pleasure. Sex manuals or feminist tracts which imply the infinite plasticity of position and pleasure, which counsel assertiveness, whether in bed or out, are dangerously destructive of imagination, of erotic and of spiritual ingenuity. The sexual exchange will be as complicated as the relationship in general – even more so.

> **Gillian Rose** (1947-1995) British philosopher, author of *Love's Work*.

Most women would rather have someone whispering their name at optimum moments than rocket with contractions to the moon.

> **Merle Shaine** (1935-1989), Canadian writer.

Consumption

The culture of consumption and the continuing crises of deprivation, with their inherent disparities, are the real-life battlegrounds of sustainable development and environmental space.

Josefa Rizalina M Bautista,
contemporary, Filipina environmentalist.

Unity

When I sleep every night,
what am I called or not called?
And when I wake, who am I
if I was not I while I slept?

This means to say that scarcely
have we landed into life
than we come as if new-born;
let us not fill our mouths
with so many faltering names,
with so many sad formalities,
with so many pompous letters,
with so much of yours and mine,
with so much signing of papers.

I have a mind to confuse things,
unite them, bring them to birth,
mix them up, undress them,
until the light of the world
has the oneness of the ocean.

Pablo Neruda (1904-1973), Chilean poet.

GNP

The gross national product includes air pollution and advertising for cigarettes, and ambulances to clear our highways of carnage. It counts special locks for our doors, and jails for people who break them. The gross national product includes the destruction of the redwoods and the death of Lake Superior. It grows with the production of napalm and missiles with nuclear warheads.

And if the gross national product includes all this, there is much that it does not comprehend. It does not allow for the health of our families, the quality of their education, or the joy of their play. It is indifferent to the decency of our factories and the safety of the streets alike. It does not include the beauty of our poetry, the intelligence of our public debate or the integrity of our public officials.

The gross national product measures neither our wit nor our courage, neither our wisdom nor our learning, neither our compassion nor our devotion to country. It measures everything, in short, except that which makes life worthwhile.

Robert Kennedy (1925-1968), US politician.

Empathy

*B*less you for your jealousy
It's a sign of empathy
(Transform the energy to admiration
and what you admire will become
part of your life)

Yoko Ono, contemporary, Japanese-born US artist.

Value

Advertising, marketing, even packaging aim at shaping people's preferences rather than, as laissez-faire theory holds, merely responding to them. Unsure of what they stand for, people increasingly rely on money as the criterion of value. What is more expensive is considered better. What used to be a medium of exchange has usurped the place of fundamental values, reversing the relationship postulated by economic theory. The cult of success has replaced a belief in principles. Society has lost its anchor.

George Soros, contemporary, Hungarian-born currency speculator and philanthropist.

Connections

At first I thought I was fighting to save the rubber trees, then I thought I was fighting to save the Amazon rainforest. Now I realize I am fighting for humanity.

Chico Mendez (1947-1988), indigenous Brazilian rubber tapper, union-leader and grassroots activist who was brutally murdered by cattle ranching interests.

Otherness

Keep cats
if you want to learn to cope with
the otherness of lovers.
Otherness is not always neglect –
Cats return to their litter trays
when they need to.

Eunice de Souza, contemporary Indian poet.

Expanding Universe

The discovery that the universe is expanding was one of the great intellectual revolutions of the twentieth century. With hindsight, it is easy to wonder why no-one had thought of it before. Newton, and others, should have realized that a static universe would soon start to contract under the influence of gravity. But suppose instead that the universe was expanding. If it was expanding fairly slowly, the force of gravity would cause it eventually to stop expanding and then to start contracting. However, if it was expanding at more than a certain critical rate, gravity would never be strong enough to stop it, and the universe would continue to expand for ever. This is a bit like what happens when one fires a rocket upward... If it has a fairly low speed, gravity will eventually stop the rocket and it will start falling back... but if the rocket has more than a certain critical speed... it will keep going way from the earth for ever.

Stephen Hawking, contemporary British physicist and author of *A Brief History of Time.*

Emotions

The heart has its reasons which reason knows nothing of.

Blaise Pascal (1623-1662), French mathematician, physicist and moralist, writing in *Pensées*.

Liberty

The only purpose for which power can rightfully be exercised over any member of a civilized community against their will is to prevent harm to others...

John Stuart Mill (1806-1873), British utilitarian philosopher, writing in *On Liberty*.

Every law is evil, for every law is an infraction of liberty.

Jeremy Bentham (1748-1832), British writer on jurisprudence and utilitarian philosopher.

Turning Point

After a time of decay comes the turning point. The powerful light that has been banished returns. There is movement but it is not brought about by force... The movement is natural, arising spontaneously. For this reason the transformation of the old becomes easy. The old is discarded and the new is introduced. Both measures accord with the time; therefore no harm results.

I Ching, Chinese book of prediction.

Sexual Difference

Sexual difference is one of the important questions of our age, if not in fact the burning issue... But wherever I turn, whether to philosophy, science or religion, I find that this underlying and increasingly insistent question remains silenced. It is as if opening up this question would allow us to put a check on the many forms of destruction in the universe...

For the work of sexual difference to take place, a revolution in thought and ethics is needed... We must reinterpret the whole relationship between subject and discourse, the subject and the world, the subject and the cosmic, the microcosmic and the macrocosmic...

Is there not still something held in reserve within the silence of female history: an energy, morphology, growth or blossoming still to come from the female realm? Such a flowering keeps the future open. The world remains uncertain in the fact of this strange event.

Luce Irigaray, contemporary, Belgian-born feminist philosopher, author of *Speculum of the Other Woman*.

Potential

Focusing your life solely on making a buck shows a certain poverty of ambition. It asks too little of yourself. Because it's only when you hitch your wagon to something larger than yourself that you realize your true potential.

Barack Obama (b 1961), first black US president.

Government

The ballot is stronger than the bullet.

Abraham Lincoln (1809-1865), American Republican President and abolitionist, who was, ironically, killed by an assassin's bullet.

Diversity

Through patents and genetic engineering, new colonies are being carved out. The land, the forests, the rivers, the oceans, and the atmosphere have all been colonized, eroded, and polluted. Capital now has to look for new colonies to invade and exploit for its further accumulation. These new colonies are, in my view, the interior spaces of the bodies of women, plants, and animals. Resistance to biopiracy is a resistance to the ultimate colonization of life itself – of the future evolution as well as the future of non-Western traditions of relating to and knowing nature. It is a struggle to protect the freedom of diverse species to evolve. It is a struggle to protect the freedom of diverse cultures to evolve. It is a struggle to conserve both cultural and biological diversity.

Vandana Shiva, contemporary, Indian physicist and ecologist, writing in *Biopiracy*.

Eternity

Never the spirit was born; the spirit shall cease to be never
Never was time it was not; End and Beginning are dreams!
Birthless and deathless and changeless remaineth the spirit for ever.

The Bhagavad Gita (c 500 BC), a poem from the *Mahabharata*, one of the most widely studied sacred writings of Hinduism.

One dies only once and it's for such a long time!

Molière (1622-1673), French comic playwright.

Communication

I distrust the incommunicable: it is the source of all violence.

Jean-Paul Sartre (1905-1980),
French philosopher and writer.

Silence is vanity, speak for the whole truth's sake.

Steve Smith (1902-1971), British poet,
novelist and illustrator.

Fear

It is not power that corrupts but fear. Fear of losing power corrupts those who wield it and the fear of the scourge of power corrupts those who are subject to it. Most Burmese are familiar with the four *a-gati*, the four kinds of corruption. *Chanda-gati*, corruption induced by desire, is deviation from the right path in pursuit of bribes or for the sake of those one loves. *Dosa-gati* is taking the wrong path in spite of those against whom one bears ill will, and *moha-gati* is aberration due to ignorance. But perhaps the worst of the four is *bhaya-gati*, for not only does *bhaya*, fear, stifle and slowly destroy all sense of right and wrong, it so often lies at the root of the other three kinds of corruption.

Aung San Suu Kyi, contemporary, human-rights activist and democratic leader of Burma, writing in *Freedom from Fear*. She has been detained by the ruling military junta since 1989.

To the Point

*B*revity is the sister of talent.

Anton Chekhov (1860-1904), Russian playwright
and medical doctor.

About the New Internationalist

New Internationalist is a publications co-operative based in Oxford, UK, with editorial and sales offices in New Zealand/Aotearoa, Australia and Canada.

It publishes the **New Internationalist** magazine on global issues, which has 65,000 subscribers worldwide. The NI also produces the One World Calendar, Almanac and Greetings Cards, as well as publications such as *Yasuní Green Gold* and food books including *Street Food* and *Vegetarian Quick & Easy* - cooking from around the world.

For more information write to:

Aotearoa/New Zealand PO Box 35038, Christchurch. newint@chch. planet.org.nz

Australia and PNG 28 Austin Street, Adelaide 5000, South Australia. helenp@newint.com.au

Canada and US 401 Richmond Street West, Studio 393, Toronto, Ontario M5V 3A8. nican@web.ca

United Kingdom 55 Rectory Road, Oxford OX4 1BW. ni@newint.org

Visit the **NI** website at **www.newint.org**

THE LITTLE BOOK OF AFRICAN WISDOM
Proverbs from Africa and the Caribbean

Collected by PATRICK IBEKWE

'Do not blame God for having created the tiger, but thank him for not having given it wings.' Amharic/Ethiopia

'He who loves, loves you with your dirt.' Uganda

'Hate people, but don't give them baskets to fetch water in.' Trinidad

No great deeds, works of art or books of history reveal so much about a culture as the folklore and collective wisdom of its sayings. All over Africa, and throughout the Caribbean and the United States there is a rich and robust oral black tradition which has been lovingly collected by **PATRICK IBEKWE** in this book. The quotations are attractively presented on the page with a range of designs, motifs, sculptures and carvings which pick up on the sentiments expressed. Easy to browse through, this book is an inspiration for lessons, speeches or articles and for all lovers of African culture.

from New Internationalist Publications **www.newint.org**

ISBN 978-1-906523-20-6

THE LITTLE BOOK OF GREAT WOMEN
Thoughts from women who changed the world

Forget 'Little Women'. Forget demure damsels, neatly tucked into the mental corsets of patriarchy. This is the book of women who challenged and changed the world. The Great Women we mean range from Hypatia to Goldman; de Beauvoir to Roy; Allende to el Saadawi. Enjoy the thoughts, deeds and exploits of women who have made their mark and those who continue to do so.

A truly international little book, including a good selection of often under-represented African, Latin American, Asian and African-American women of note.

◆ User-friendly
◆ Small in size but large enough in subject matter to fully engage the grey cells.
◆ Ideal for the busy person with more brain than time.

ISBN 978-1-906523-22-0
See all our products on the NI website at **www.newint.org**